USE YOUR HEAD, DEAR

BY

ALIKI

GREENWILLOW BOOKS

NEW YORK

C.4

Library of Congress Cataloging in Publication Data
Aliki.   Use your head, dear.
Summary: Charles, a young alligator, means well,
but gets things mixed up until his father gives
him an invisible thinking cap for his birthday.
[1. Alligators—Fiction]   I. Title.
PZ7.A397Us   1983   [E]   82-11911
ISBN 0-688-01811-4
ISBN 0-688-01812-2 (lib. bdg.)

for Christina
and Diana

Fifteen doves stood by the garden door,
waiting to be fed.
"Oh dear," said Mother. "Charles
forgot again."

On good days, Charles brushed his teeth
instead of his back,

went out the door instead of the window,
and put Minnie back in her cage
when he finished playing with her.

But on bad days, if Mother said,
"Charles, dear, please take this
sandwich to Father,"
Minnie got the cheese,

the doves got the bread,
and Father was left with the dish.

On bad days, Charles didn't get
anything right.
"Even baby Marsha knows where
the dust pan belongs," said Mother,
closing the refrigerator door.
"Please use your head, dear,
you are a big boy now.
You're starting school next week."

"I can't wait," he said, when the day came.
"It will be fun," said Mother.
"You will paint and sculpt and build."

Charles loved every minute of it.
He built with paints, sculpted the soap,
and painted the blocks.

"Story time," said Miss Crock.
The children gathered around her.
When she had finished reading,
she noticed Charles.
"Someone is asleep on the floor,"
she said.
"Charles," called the children.
"Wake up!"
Charles woke up.
"Are you tired, Charles?" asked
Miss Crock.
"No, not a bit."
"Then why were you sleeping?"
"I always sleep when Mother reads
me a bedtime story."
"This isn't bedtime, Charles."

The children had their milk and cookies.
Then it was rest time.
"Charles, would you please close the
curtains?"
asked Miss Crock.
"I'd love to," said Charles.

On his way back, he knocked down
the blocks, kicked over a pot, and
stepped on Martin's toe.
"I got lost in the dark," said Charles.
"That's enough for one day." Miss Crock
sighed.

"How was school?" asked Mother.

"Fun!" said Charles. "They kept me busy."

Charles and Marsha played until
dinnertime.
"Oh, there's the phone," said Mother.
"Please help Marsha with her
spaghetti, Charles. And I mean
Marsha, dear. Not Minnie
or Cheeky or the doves."

Charles helped Marsha with her spaghetti.
He braided it on her head and tied it up
in ribbons.

"I don't know what we're going to do
with you, Charles," Mother said,
when she came back.
"I told you to use your head."
"I'm sorry, Mother," he said.
"You asked me to help."

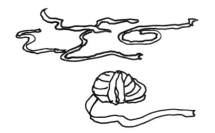

"All right, dear," said Mother wearily.
"It's late now. Get in the bathtub
and I'll be right up."
When Mother got there, Charles was
in the empty tub, sound asleep.

"You look tired, Mother," said Father.
"I'm not only tired," said Mother. "I'm
exhausted, done in, and near collapse."
"I think you've already collapsed,"
said Father.

"It's Charles," said Mother. "He doesn't
keep his mind on what he's doing.
He's dear and sweet and means well, but
with Charles everything gets mixed up,
or forgotten. We have to do something."

"You have a point," said Father. "But we ought to be patient. Remember all the trouble we had when he was younger, and never kept his mouth closed, and ate all the wrong things? Well, he got over that. He'll learn."

"I don't know if I can wait that long," said Mother, "but I'll try."

In the next few weeks, Mother tried
to help Charles.
She tied strings around his fingers
and toes, to help him remember.

She hung signs from his hat.

She tied a knot in his tail.
"Maybe this will help,"
she said hopefully.
But it didn't.

One day soon after, Mother burst into
Charles's room.

"Happy birthday, Charles!" she said. "Today
is your day. Let's get ready for the party."
They cleaned the house.

They baked a cake, and got the
pizzas ready.

Charles was resting when Father came
in with a big box.
"Happy birthday, Charles," he said.
Charles opened it expectantly.
There was nothing inside.
"It's an invisible thinking cap," said Father.
"It's impossible to lose, and once you
put it on, it always works. I know.
I've worn mine for years."

"Thank you, Father," said Charles.
He put on the thinking cap,
admired it in the mirror,
and ran to answer the door.

"Happy birthday, Charles,"
said all his friends.
They played games, and laughed,
and made a lot of noise.
They ate their pizzas and drank
all their apple juice.
"Now open your presents!" said all
the children excitedly.

Martin gave him a pair of sunglasses.

"Now I won't get lost in the dark," said Charles.

Stella gave him a compass.

"Now I'll know which way to go!" he said.

Noel gave him a ruler.

"Now I'll know how long to stay." He laughed.

Helen gave him stacking cups.

"Now I can sort out the pet food," he exclaimed.

Canio gave him a book.

"I'll read it before I go to sleep," he said.

Marsha held out a package.
In it was a ball of twine.
"Now we can do the spaghetti trick
without spaghetti," he said.

Mother gave him a watch.

"Waterproof!" said Charles.

"I can even wear it when I remember
to fill the tub."

Everyone clapped to see the big cake.
"Make a wish," said Martin.
"I don't know what," said Charles.
"Use your head, dear," said Mother.
"That's it!" said Charles.
He blew out all the candles
in one breath.

"Now your wish will come true,"
said Marsha.
"It already has," said Charles.

yoo hoo

When ALIKI is not slaving away at her desk,
or cooking up a storm for her husband and
children, she is digging in her garden among
the three hundred tulips (which come up to her
surprise), hoping against hope she won't
stumble against an earthworm.